Praise for the Graduate/Stu Coach

Companies

Jeff Fugler – CEO – The Charlotte Street Agency

"We have regularly taken on interns via Graduate Coach and have always found them to be of the highest standard. One advantage of hiring via Graduate Coach is that in every instance we have found them ready to hit the ground running. We have had no need to train them further. We have literally been able to throw them in the deep end."

"The money we have saved as a business this way has been considerable, never mind the saving in time as well. We would have no hesitation in recommending their services to any parent or Graduate."

"In fact, I have sent two graduates to them for Coaching, so impressed have I been with the quality of coaching they receive."

Ben Norton – Commercial Director – ICP

"I would have no hesitation in recommending Chris and Graduate Coach for any organisation."

"Given a short lead time and a skeletal project outline Chris quickly provided two well-briefed young graduates that possessed the IQ/EQ you hope for. They and he were a pleasure to work with and I would have no hesitation in recommending Chris and Graduate Coach for any organisation seeking intelligent, capable and diligent interns – excellent service."

Jeremy Prescot – Deputy Chairman 2112 Communications

"I have known Chris as a business colleague and friend since 1976 when I joined what was then the best advertising agency in the UK – Collett Dickenson and Pearce (CDP)."

"Chris was my first manager there and I worked closely with him for the next twelve years. During that time (and since) he has always demonstrated many qualities. He is inspiring, diligent, clever, creative and very loyal to everyone with whom he works. Above all, he has extraordinary drive to succeed for himself and all his clients."

"When my son needed mentoring because he had no idea what career he wished to pursue, I had no hesitation in asking Chris to help him. He suggested opportunities, coached him, helped him create an effective CV and helped him to get and prepare him for interviews, and finally helped land a really good job."

"I heartily recommend Chris and Graduate Coach."

Graduates

Saul P

"Following months of feeling lost and depressed about my future career prospects, meeting Chris was a turning point. He helped to identify my strengths and key personality traits which I, like most people of my age, was totally oblivious to."

"If you have recently started working or are stuck in your career, give the book a read: you'll be surprised by how helpful it will be."

Andrew B

"Chris helped to transform my career and my life. Within a few hours of meeting him he'd identified the perfect-fit sector for me, and after a bit of CV and interview technique work I found a job in an industry I'd never have gone for myself. I made the jump from having a dead-end job as a waiter to working a full-time role in digital marketing in less than a month."

Simon

"With his help I refined my interview skills"

"Chris is an excellent coach. Working with him was a real pleasure because I could sense his passion and enthusiasm for what he does. With his help I refined my interview skills and my first interview, after only one week with him, was a huge success. Due to his extensive work experience and unique insights in the field of marketing, he could give me a lot of good advice on how I can stay on top of my industry."

Susan

"...the most helpful thing was the ability and confidence that I was given to answer the hundreds of competency questions that I encountered at phone interview, assessment days and final interviews."

Alex

"I would recommend Graduate Coach to anyone looking to receive coaching as a graduate, something that is not easy to find, with such relevance and quality."

Emma J

"Thanks to Chris' years of advertising experience... he was able to advise me on the best approach."

Alex A

"Chris Davies is sparklingly intelligent, and sharply perceptive. He has a brilliant knack for understanding the talents and drives of others (which they themselves might not know) and the experience and know-how for getting that first foot in the door. I would urge anyone who is feeling lost since leaving education to pick up this book. You may be surprised at where it takes you."

THE
GRADUATE
BOOK

AUSTIN MACAULEY PUBLISHERS™

LONDON • CAMBRIDGE • NEW YORK • SHARJAH

For those wanting to create a successful future for themselves.

THE GRADUATE BOOK

All you need to know to do really well at work

CHRIS DAVIES
Graduate Coach

A CIP catalogue record for this title is available from the British Library.

ISBN 9781788785228 (Paperback)
ISBN 9781788785235 (E-Book)
www.austinmacauley.com

First Published (2018)
Austin Macauley Publishers Ltd™
25 Canada Square
Canary Wharf
London
E14 5LQ

Contents

Contents

Foreword

Geoff Howard-Spink

I got a call in July from Chris Davies. He asked if I would write an introduction to a book he was publishing.

We hadn't spoken for years. More like decades actually. I was intrigued. Flattered as well, and impressed by the fact that Chris had tracked me down. So I agreed. See Chapter 7 – The seventh key: Build networks and make friends.

Chris sent me the manuscript and I immediately saw that many of the Thirteen Keys matched my own working life experience.

My best boss was Stanley Pollit, founder of Boase Massimi Pollit. I worked at two legendary Advertising Agencies in succession: BMP followed by Collett Dickenson Pearce. Tick Keys 4 and 5.

Resilience is a quality that can be acquired. Had to be in my case. In advertising it's an essential survival skill. Just being smart and well prepared isn't always enough to prevail. Running marathons helped me. Tick Key 6 and maybe Key 8 as well.

I scraped a pass in O Level maths and got a degree in economics without ever understanding a formula. But I did get the significance of numbers. I learned that from Stanley Pollitt. Don't believe that the world now belongs to the quants, but don't skip over the tables in a document either. Tick Key 9.

My first job was a trainee at Lintas. At the time it was Unilever's in-house agency. The nice ladies that looked after the trainees fixed me up with an elocution coach to iron out the north-west London accent. After the first session I agreed with the coach, an actor, that we'd spend the hour a week talking about films and skip the elocution bit. Tick Key 11.

Although In the mid-1960s when I was looking for my first job it was a lot easier than it is today, I suspect that the transition from education to paid employment was as difficult then as it is now.

I didn't have a coach like Chris to mentor and advise me. Such people didn't exist then. But what I can say is that my lived experience endorses what a graduate will find in this book.

Preface

It has come as a complete joy to me to discover that coaching people is the very best job I have ever had. I had no idea when I started out as a young graduate trainee that trying to help other people would enthral me so much.

I have helped many people develop the skills and confidence they need to land really good jobs. I have learnt much along the way – and I am still learning – but one thing has become increasingly clear: it's great to help someone land a job, but then what? Where do you go from there?

That's why I felt the need to write a book. While there are hundreds of books and YouTube videos on how to get a job, there are few that guide you once you have one. And my intuition is that many of us would wish that we had such a guide, because the transition to work is often difficult. I was completely bewildered by it for at least the first year and frankly not much good to anyone during my second year.

Years later, I began to wonder why I was so useless in the beginning. Eventually I realised why: I had come from the usual school and university environment where people were paid to help me learn and develop. Then I was employed by a very large, successful and benevolent employer where I was largely expected to work out things for myself. I was suddenly on my own, with at least 10 problems a day to deal with and the same number of decisions to make.

Nowadays, nothing has changed. All employers pay lip service to the need to coach and mentor, and most will try to help, but bosses and leaders will always have their hands full. When I was running a company, I reckon that I had to make at least 15 decisions a day. Helping new hires (especially those fresh from university) is only – and will only ever be – a very small part of an employer's daily preoccupation.

That is the reality of working life.

You will come to realise that you are now, for the first time in your life, completely responsible for you. There is nobody being paid to hold your hand to help you learn. You have to learn by yourself. You are the one person who will decide the long-term fate of your career.

Although I did have help from some great bosses, (and that will be a key message in this book – find a great boss) most of what I learnt along the way I did by myself, and always from making mistakes.

As this realisation began to take shape in my head, I began to imagine what would have happened to me if there had been a book I could have read to coach me. It would have been a much less bumpy ride for a start. I would have saved myself hundreds, possibly thousands, of hours of wasted effort. Therefore, this is my hope: that by reading this book you will save yourself a huge amount of time and wasted effort and will learn and keep learning faster and more productively. The mastery of any cognitively demanding job always is a long and sometimes arduous task. I also hope that by telling my story of how I made it (from very inauspicious beginnings) you will get to your 'where you want to be' more quickly and with much less trauma.

Nowadays, 'going on a journey' is a cliché, but in this context, it makes sense to use it. Your working life really will be a journey, and it will last at least 50 years.

People almost gasp when they first hear that, however, this is the average number of years a young adult is likely to work before they retire. People rarely think about it this way at the start of their working lives.

Given the length of time you will be working, if you can find work that fulfils you then that journey will be so much more enjoyable.

But what makes for fulfilling work? It is very simple: work where you are able to develop your skills. The continual acquisition and mastery of new, work-based skills (so different from those academic ones learnt at school and university) will also help you develop your self-esteem and mark your final accession to adulthood. That is the way to find fulfilment at work. In this book, we are going to look at what these skills are and how to develop them.

So enjoy! I hope you find the book interesting and, above all, useful.

Chris Davies

Acknowledgements

Firstly, I want to thank Kirsty Ellen Smillie and her team at Austin Macauley. They were the first publishers who said, "Yes, these two books work together and should be published as a pair".

Every other publisher thought I was crazy. Time will tell!

I also want to thank my best boss, Geoff Howard-Spink. It only really dawned me when I started coaching how lucky I was to have had such a great mentor.

He gave me my first break into Senior Management when he asked me to start a new advertising agency, CDP/Aspect, for Collet Dickerson and Pearce (CDP) when I was 27. His patience during that first traumatic year when we pitched 22 times and only won four accounts was nothing short of miraculous!

After that rocky start (it's described more fully in The Graduate Book) we went on to great things and the original band of six eventually became 150.

I will never forget those days; we were never the most talented bunch but we were one of the hardest working, and we always worked as a team. It is impossible to personally thank everyone but these folk were the backbone of the company – Barbara Harrison, Karen Pursey, Nick Mann, John Mundy, Robin Murtough, Jeremy Prescot, Mark Robinson and Douglas Seddon.

Since those advertising years, I have worked with many other talented people. Peter Gordon, Denise Roberts and David Taylor have been instrumental in the growth of Graduate Coach.

Carole Norris taught me so much especially about how to coach and how best to help students on the autistic spectrum.

In addition, I have asked for help from my mentoring team of Brian Berg, Jeff Fugler, Jeremy Prescot and Gary Trueman many times over the last seven years. They have been great cheerleaders for Graduate Coach, always encouraging me when times were tough, which they were in the early days.

These two books have been a team effort as well. Denise Roberts, Mike Everett and Bernadette Williams have helped me write them, Bridget Wilkins has been a very patient copy editor/proof reader and Ian Kingston has done a fine job on the book designs. Thanks also to Jeff Fugler and Jon White for their kind introductions and to John Mundy for his photography.

I need to thank Bruce Woodcock of the Careers and Employability team from the University of Kent for permission to adapt a number of charts from their careers website. It's an excellent free resource that any student can use. Data, charts and statistics from High Fliers Research have also been invaluable to this project.

Graduate Coach itself only exists because of all those clients who have put their faith in me. I owe them all so much.

I have learnt and am still learning so much about how best to help young people succeed in this very competitive world, and sometimes I feel that they are teaching me.

I learnt a lot in all those advertising years about how to sell products and at times it was very satisfying, especially when I was working for smaller brands who were up against big corporations, but it's nothing like the feeling I get when somebody I have coached succeeds in landing a job.

It's certainly the best job I have ever had. And for that I am truly blessed.

Last but not least, I know I could never have succeeded in this and the other careers I have had over these past years without the unflagging support of my wife, Mariel.

When we first met, she was a successful young dentist and I was a struggling young advertising man. But she believed in me then as she believes in me now.

We all need someone we can lean on and I have always leant on her.

Chris Davies

Introduction

Starting Out

From my earliest days at school to the time I started work I felt intellectually inferior to my peers. Somehow, they appeared to be brighter, better educated and more articulate than I was. I found that the only way I could compete with them was to work harder.

But it was when I took up my first job that the need to work harder hit me hardest. In those days, the early seventies, advertising was a highly sought-after career and was therefore particularly adept at attracting the brightest minds. In the main, these brainboxes were recruited from Oxford and Cambridge. It astonished me how they were able to grasp complex ideas quickly, and explain them simply and succinctly.

I felt like a dunce in their presence.

However, as time went by, a change took place and I began to out-perform my peers. I didn't realise it at the time, but I'd discovered the art of working smarter. By adopting a specific set of actions, I was marshalling an arsenal of skills that were helping me to carve out a successful career. I was beginning to manage the transition from university to work. At the same time, I was future proofing my skills.

How I progressed past my peers

My story begins in the spring of 1972. I was about to graduate but I was clueless as to what I wanted to do next. Despite having studied biology for three years, I knew I didn't want to be a biologist. I was fed up with the subject. On the other hand, I had enjoyed being a student leader for the university's Rag Week and had loved running the hall of residence's bar committee. I'd also had a ball when I was selected to become the first student representative on the university's board of governors. But still, I had no idea what to do as a career.

One day I got chatting to my next-door neighbour in halls. He was studying marketing and appeared never to work that hard. He lent me some of his textbooks. One weekend I settled down with one and read it from cover to cover. Boy, did it leave an impression. It's a book that I will always remember and it remains the definitive textbook in its field: *Kotler on Marketing*.

This book introduced me to a whole new world of brands and advertising. This world struck me as fascinating; perhaps more usefully, it seemed to me that it might be a world in which I could flourish. I had worked in shops since I was a kid, to top up my pocket money. Many of the strategies and tips offered by the book seemed to embody much of the common sense that the shopkeepers for whom I worked practised daily. Things like being mindful of your best customers; making sure you know who those customers are; not discounting unless there was no alternative; and discovering what people want you to sell them, and selling them that; and so on.

So I set out to become a marketing executive. Along the way, a human resources executive from Dunlop, the tyre manufacturer, interviewed me at a recruitment event at university. He told me that he thought I was better suited to advertising than marketing.

Subsequently he wrote to me suggesting the names of some advertising agencies I might approach. What I didn't realise at the time was that they were all agencies that did work for Dunlop. The power of patronage being what it was back then meant that at the very least I would have been granted an interview if I told them that someone from Dunlop had encouraged me to apply for a job with them.

However, after five rejection letters (biologists weren't top of advertising agencies' hire lists in those days, whereas arts graduates from Oxford and Cambridge were) I wasn't so much disheartened as even more determined to learn all I could about advertising.

I read everything I could lay my hands on. The more I read, the more fascinated I became – and the more determined. Then, one day, The Times newspaper carried a competition that was being run by J. Walter Thompson — at that time, London's number one advertising agency. I entered and was invited for an interview.

To their eternal credit, despite having rejected me initially, they granted me a place on the graduate selection process: six gruelling interviews.

Together with another applicant, an Oxford graduate, I was hired. I was the first-ever non- Oxbridge graduate to be given a management trainee job by J. Walter Thompson. Suddenly, a whole new and exciting world opened up before me.

At first I floundered. I had been a top dog at university and now had to get used to life at the bottom of the food chain.

Even more worrying was that most of the people that surrounded me seemed to be formidably bright. I felt unable even to begin to match their intellects.

After a difficult 18 months, I was headhunted by one of J. Walter Thompson's competitors, Collett, Dickenson, Pearce and Partners (CDP). This agency was at the cutting edge of creativity and, although it had a fair number of Oxbridge men, it also employed non-graduates from working class backgrounds such as mine on its staff.

At CDP my ethos of working harder really came into its own. I did more work than any of my contemporaries. I learnt that hard work meant I could match their output.

Every weekend I would avidly read documents that other account managers would lend me.

Eventually, it sunk in that I was starting to learn. The harder I worked the more I learnt. And the more I learnt, the more successful I became, and the happier and more fulfilled I felt. I read more than my peers. I noticed that often they would talk, rather than listen. Which to me didn't make sense.

After seven years, when I was only 28, CDP asked me to start a second advertising agency, CDP Aspect, to mop up business that the main agency was unable to handle. Four years later, I bought it out with seven others.

At that time the management buy-out of CDP Aspect was the largest-ever to have taken place in London advertising.

I successfully sold it seven years later, just after I had turned 35.

As *Campaign*, the advertising trade magazine, reported in December 1982, I had gone in as something akin to the "joint post of captain, groundsman and turnstile operator" at an unknown football club and emerged like a player joining the Premier League.

What had I done? And how did I do it? Not just through hard work, but hard work combined with purposeful learning. I had become successful by working hard and learning to be smart. I learnt to grow in the skills that would help me to be fulfilled and to succeed. This had allowed me to achieve more than my peers. I had proved that it doesn't matter where or how you start; it doesn't matter if people around you are better educated or brighter. What matters is making the most of the abilities you've been given.

What experts say about working smart

Malcolm Gladwell, the speaker and bestselling author, puts working smart into context this way: "In cognitively demanding fields there are no naturals. Nobody walks into an operating room straight out of medical school and does world-class neurosurgery."

No one is born a great surgeon. A surgeon develops the skills to become great through sheer hard work and gritted determination. He or she develops these skills by continually learning, revising, adapting, and repeating these actions time and time again.

This was exactly what I had done, though I hadn't realised it at the time.

I had walked out of university into a job in advertising and soon twigged that my only chance of becoming successful was to work hard, smartly.

Precisely what I did and why it worked is backed up by research, research that demonstrates how, by adopting the right actions and mindset, you can determine whether you soar or sink during your first year at work – and beyond. In fact, it is research that will serve you well in all areas of your life – personal, professional, or otherwise. Take a look at these examples:

◆ Geoffrey Colvin, in his book *Talent is Overrated*, discovered that people who rise to the top in their professions aren't necessarily the most talented; instead it is those who practise their skills diligently over many years with the intention of developing those skills to a standard of excellence. The also-rans remain 'just okay', the fate that befell most of my peers. They get by, but never do anything noteworthy, nor do they get noticed.

◆ K Anders Ericsson, a Swedish sports psychologist, was the first to tell us that if you wish to master a skill you must continuously practise it for 10,000 hours, or nearly three hours a day for 10 years. That's how long researchers believe it takes for the brain to create the strong neural connections needed if you are to become a genuine expert. Ericsson says, "Experts are always made, not born." Likewise, I had invested my 10,000 hours to master being an advertising executive and it had paid off.

◆ Stanford psychologist Carol Dweck has helped us to an understanding of how even the simplest of our beliefs can affect profoundly what we get out of life. It's all down to your mindset. If you believe that your character, intelligence and creative abilities are largely static and fixed, and cannot be altered, they will remain so. See yourself as work in progress, believe that you can grow and develop your skills, and that's exactly what will happen. Your mindset determines your actions and can help you overcome hard knocks and setbacks, all of which will hone and shape your skills.

◆ Angela Duckworth's work focuses on 'grit' – the mindset that enables a person never to give up, but to keep at a task until they succeed at it. Grit is different from self-control, which enables you to achieve short-term goals. Grit is the ability that will help you endure the long haul, to keep working when at first something doesn't succeed. It is the ability to learn from failure and bounce back from it, using your experiences as stepping-stones that will guide you to where you want to go.

◆ William James (1842–1910) is noted for first using the term 'plasticity' in 1890 to refer to behaviour. But since then scores of scientists have contributed to the knowledge that our brains can change and grow new connections, throughout our entire lives. This is what's now known as Neuroplasticity, a term that describes what happens to our brains when we learn: how the brain processes information, turns that into memory, and eventually transforms this into knowledge and insight. It does this by firing up neurons in the area of the brain responsible for the task in hand. As they fire up, they create connections with nearby neurons, forming what might be described as mapping or wiring. The more we practise a task, the stronger the firing and wiring becomes, creating neural pathways in our brain that make it much easier to undertake a task that we once found difficult.

◆ Alan Rusbridger, previously editor of *The Guardian*, charts his step-by-step experience of learning how to expertly play the piano in his excellent book, *Play It Again*. In an interview with Ray Dolan, professor of neuropsychiatry at UCL and a pioneer of neurobehavioral research, Rusbridger asked, "What takes place in the brain as one becomes better skilled?" Dolan explained how, through practice, we move our skill from explicit memory (memory that's more easily recalled) to the deeper procedural type memory (memory that becomes subconscious and therefore not so easily recalled). This type of memory develops from the experience of learning everything we do, from riding a bike to writing a letter. Once we develop behavioural fluency in this skill it becomes a procedural memory or skill. The process of how this occurs is intriguing: the neurons in that area of our brain grow dendrites – little threads at the top of the neuron that sprout and enable it to make connections with other neurons – when we begin to learn something new. Through continuous practice of the skill, the dendrites become thicker and we become proficient at that skill.

We will return to this research later.

Developing the skills I needed to reach the top in my field was hard. As the research I have quoted demonstrates, becoming an expert takes work, lots of it. I suffered many ups and downs, twists and turns, and failures along the way. I made many mistakes, but I learnt from them and eventually, hard work and gritty determination began to pay off.

The intention of this book is to show you what I did and how I did it. Why? Because I want you be able to emulate my experience and develop the skills that will propel you to fulfilment. This is an exciting time in your life. The things I am about to tell you are the things I wish somebody had told me when I started out. It would have saved me a lot of time.

Below are listed the 13 Keys that helped me become successful at work. Employ these in the days, months and years ahead and they will help you become expert at what you do. Study them carefully.

Chapter 1
The First Key: Keep a Journal

Focus on the journey, not the destination. Joy is found not in finishing an activity but in doing it.

Greg Anderson

What's covered?

◆ Use a journal to record key learning moments along the way so as to gain the most from them.

◆ Aim to get better at doing a task rather than simply to get the task done.

◆ Create 'mental models' that show how your job fits into the bigger picture.

There's this scene in the movie *I, Robot* (starring Will Smith as detective Del Spooner) where Sonny the Robot stands on a hill overlooking the Lake Michigan landscape. For miles and miles in front of him, thousands of robots stand and stare back at him. It's a picture of hope, expectation and uncertainty as they look to Sonny to lead them into a new future never before experienced.

Starting your working life is a bit like that. It's like standing on the proverbial hill overlooking the landscape that is the new world of work. You have this new terrain lying ahead of you

– one that is huge, exciting and scary. There will be days of triumph and days of defeat as you become increasingly proficient at your job and in the world of work. There will be many diversions and pitfalls for the unwary. Learning how to effectively and successfully find your way through is probably the greatest intellectual and psychological challenge you will ever face. The test of success lies in personal satisfaction, and this is priceless.

If, for you, it feels like navigating an unknown country, then this is the map that will show you how to get from Point A to Point Z. It will be your own pocket navigator telling you where to turn and what to look out for. Like the map, it is not the territory but it will help you find career fulfilment a whole lot more quickly, more easily and in a way that is less painful than trying to work it out alone. It will help you to start off with the right attitude and to develop the right skills. It will explain the things expected of you along the way but which no one tells you because they expect you to work it out for yourself.

Before you do anything, get yourself a journal. It's an essential tool for the journey you are about to take. Write down observations about your learning on a weekly basis. The act of writing will help your brain crystallise and retain the thoughts you are recording. It will also give you the chance to look back and review your progress. When you see how much you have learned you will be motivated to keep moving forward.

Keeping a journal is at the heart of continual learning. It corresponds to Colvin's idea of deliberate practice of the skills you wish to develop. Deliberate practice, he explains, is "activity that's explicitly intended to improve performance, that reaches for objectives just beyond one's level of competence, provides feedback on results, and involves high levels of repetition".

Your journal will be complicit in this work. You will use it to break down whatever you are learning into its component parts, enabling you to practise and improve each element. As well as noting learning goals, use your journal to analyse your progress, or lack of it, and to record feedback on what you've learned from others, as well as yourself.

Colvin says that the most effective way to engage in deliberate practice is to aim to get better at performing a task, rather than just simply to get that task done. This will take lots of patient repetition as you practise the same actions over and again, observing what you learned each time.

You can also use your journal to record things you've read concerning your job or industry – these might include key names, dates and events, plus other related factors that might impact your career. Again, writing these down will help with memory and recall of the information when you need it.

Finally, the journal will assist in the creation of what researchers term 'mental models'. These are effectively maps that demonstrate how your job fits into your department, how your department operates within the company, and how the company operates within the industry. They are pictures of how all the elements fit together, and the influence they have on one another. Thus, by seeing the whole picture, you will gain a better understanding of what you are doing, and be able to decide where it might be possible for you to make meaningful contributions.

Once you have your journal, you will be ready to move on to the next 12 Keys.

Exercise 1: Keep a journal

We learn most effectively when we engage all senses, so add visual aids like diagrams and different colours to capture at least part of your learning journey.

When learning, follow a process like this:

1. Note down the skill you'd like to improve (master one skill at a time).

2. Break it down into its component parts and work on improving each step. For example, to present well you need to master body language, delivery, content and structure.

3. Practice each part.

4. Get feedback but also do your own reflecting. What went well? What needs improving. Make notes.

5. Apply what you've learned to your next presentation.

6. Repeat the process.

Chapter 2

The Second Key: Take Responsibility for Your Own Development

You cannot escape the responsibility of tomorrow by evading it today.

Abraham Lincoln

What's covered?

◆ There is only so much your company or boss can do to help you get ahead.

◆ No one can possess greater knowledge of, take greater interest in, or make a greater investment in your personal development than you.

◆ You must find the happy medium between meeting your own personal development needs and acquiring the skills needed for the job.

It is essential that you take ownership of your own learning and growth. And make no mistake, in your first job, that's no mean task. You will need to develop a completely new set of skills and use them in a brand new environment, one that's radically different from university. You'll probably find yourself working with the widest array of people you've ever encountered, people of all classes, ages and abilities, some of whom are likely to be far brighter than you are. So make sure you learn from them.

Naturally, all companies have a vested interest in the career development of their staff but it's not the job of the company to babysit or spoon-feed their employees. The relationship between employer and employee differs greatly from the relationship between teacher and student or between parent and child. Your boss's motivations aren't the same as those of teachers or lecturers, who strive to keep their students' scores high, so as to achieve high ranking in league tables. Neither do bosses form emotional attachments to those they hire. Employees who underperform are soon replaced. The fact is, that there's only so much an employer is willing or even able to do. They may place opportunities in your path but it's your responsibility, as the employee, to exploit them to the full.

In one sense, my innate need to push myself to outperform those around me drove me to take ownership of my learning very early on. I have already mentioned that I floundered in my first job at the well-known advertising agency, J. Walter Thompson. I worked on the Persil washing powder account and made no impact whatsoever throughout my first nine months. I was struggling to get used to the idea of working for a living and the need to perform well in a pressurised, corporate and competitive environment. Unlike at school or university, in the workplace you are left pretty much on your own. It was reading relevant books, asking questions, and learning from the talented people that surrounded me, that allowed me to begin to improve my skills. Soon I started to know facts and figures that my colleagues didn't. I even began to develop insights that had eluded my bosses. And that's how I came to be headhunted by Collett, Dickenson and Pearce.

A colleague I had worked with at J. Walter Thompson recommended me to the bosses at CDP after he had moved there.

Years later, in a trade magazine article about my buyout of CDP Aspect, Geoff Howard-Spink, my boss at CDP, said he had never forgotten his interview with me. He told the magazine, "Chris raised the topic of potential growth for advertising in new areas and he didn't just mention the usual things that everyone knew about. I thought it was very impressive for a guy who had been in the business for only 18 months."

I continued to improve by developing a healthy curiosity in my field and by persisting in my habit of taking responsibility for my own learning. You must also do this.

Today's environment is different to the one in which I started work. Information has increased, is far more accessible and is coming at you in data loads every second. Taking responsibility for your own learning is therefore more important today than ever because you have much more information competing for your attention.

Richard Dealtry, writing about the savvy learner in the *Journal of Workplace Learning*, describes today's work environment as one that is rich in learning opportunity. This richness has the potential to deliver you a better quality of life; one in which you are armed with the information you need to make the kind of informed decisions that lead you to become better off. But, he warns, you have to direct its course. The myriad choices, dynamics and timings can produce so many variations of outcomes that, if left to chance, you can easily succumb to the diversions and pitfalls of the unwary. The most convenient action to take isn't necessarily always the most beneficial one for you.

For the ambitious graduate embarking on this pathway, the acquisition of the right capabilities and acumen is not one that should be left to chance. Finding what Dealtry calls the right 'acumen formula' requires focus and the right deployment of your energy and time.

Your starting place is in the dependent and passive learning of university where you were told what to learn and when to learn it. The only question you needed to ask here was, "What shall I learn?"

Now in the working environment, you must break out of this unconstructive phase. You must ask, "How will what I learn help me to do my job better?" You must choose wisely how to invest your time.

Many people never manage to achieve anything great in life because they never move beyond this dependent learning stage. Perhaps no one told them. Perhaps they've never managed to work it out. Or perhaps they're simply comfortable here. Whichever it is, this is not the path you want to take.

Having left university, your first goal now is competency and eventually mastery. It is the road to maturity in learning that is much more specific to your career transition.

There are two other important points you need to grasp as to why taking responsibility for your own development is key.

First, the organisation you are working for will also have their own learning goals for you. This is basically stuff your boss will want you to learn to help the company meet its targets. Here is where the company's priorities will meet with your personal learning needs. You must find the happy middle ground between what you need to learn to develop yourself and to do your job well, and what the company needs you to learn for its own purposes. Finding this balance will also enable you to meet the needs of colleagues, customers and suppliers. It will also help you create a better balance between your personal and working life.

The second point I want you to remember is that your starting place to developing yourself will be different to anyone else's, so never compare yourself, even to someone else doing the same job.

This is because the route you take will depend on where you came from: your family background, education, work experience and social activities will have influenced and shaped your world outlook. Use them to get to know yourself better and to become the best you can be. As you learn and shape your course, the result can be a career that is equally unique and immensely satisfying. You will discover new things about yourself, about the way you think and the way you work; and about your strengths and weaknesses. You will develop stronger character, leadership and social skills.

Making the most of the resources and opportunities available to you is the skill that will help you shape your own destiny. You will own your personal and unique learning processes and be well on the road to releasing your full potential.

Exercise 2: Take responsibility for your own development

1. List the skills your organisation needs you to have to do your job well. Now list those you need for your own career development. Are there any differences between the two lists?

2. Be proactive. Seek support from your manager to help you develop the skills on both lists. Find out what training events, conferences and workshops are available to help you develop these skills.

Chapter 3

The Third Key: Before All Else, Seek to Learn

You don't learn to walk by following rules. You learn by doing, and by falling over.

Richard Branson

What's covered?

◆ The first thing you need to learn when starting out in the world of work is work or soft skills.

◆ These skills include working well with others, learning how to think in a work environment, and learning to be responsible.

◆ Don't worry if your first or second job isn't the ideal position you'd like – use this time to learn and to allow your personality to develop.

What's the point of going to university? For the overwhelming majority of us it is to get a good job afterwards. The problem, however, is that university doesn't prepare you for the new world of work. You're expected to work it out for yourself, so where do you begin?

It may surprise you, but the first thing you must demonstrate to your boss from day one is that you are willing to learn. You must approach your job with the objective to learn. And you must first begin by aiming to learn 'soft' skills.

Psychologist Daniel Goleman PhD, author of the bestselling book, *Emotional Intelligence*, says that new hires often miss this important point when they first start working. They don't spend enough time developing their soft skills because they are too focused on making an impact in the job.

This is not their fault, as in my experience, very few bosses really ever spell out what they want from a new hire. And even if they do, it is rarely anything in the degree of detail a young graduate needs. Employers don't mean to do it. They're just very busy. So they sort of plonk you in the middle of the work environment to work it out for yourself.

As a result, new hires often miss opportunities to learn and develop soft skills such as getting along well with others, developing empathy and managing their own emotions. At the end, as Amy Cuddy has also highlighted in her book, *Presence*, people on internships, work experience, graduate programmes or probationary periods don't get asked to stay on because nobody got to know them. They didn't ask for help and, rather than seek first to learn, they sought first to show what they know.

There is a vast chasm between what new employees think a manager wants and what a manager actually seeks. Research shows that 90 per cent of business leaders believe that employees with strong people skills make better commercial impact; 85 per cent of business leaders believe that technical skills are essential in those they hire, but see soft skills as the characteristic that sets them apart. Those with soft skills advance faster. Technical skills will land you the job but soft skills are what will get you promoted.

Soft skills are the type that are easily transferable to any job, and they are in great demand. For example, you should:

1. Learn to be good with people. Some people have empathy coursing through their veins but most of us don't. It is, however, possible to learn to become more empathetic. And you need to, as being able to work with lots of different personality types is crucial.

2. Learn to be thorough. Most of us start on fairly menial tasks but wherever you start try to take pride in what you do. Take care over what you do and do it well. Otherwise, your boss will think you can't be bothered.

3. Learn to take responsibility. If you've been given a task, do whatever is required of you to get it done. Don't blame other people or circumstances for not meeting deadlines. If you find that there's a problem, don't shirk it. Face it and sort it out.

4. Learn how your job fits into the organisation. Who is who and what do they do? How does the marketing department work with, say, operations or production? Learn as much as possible about your organisation and your industry. Read both the trade press and the company's internal news bulletins.

5. Learn how to think logically, evidence your thoughts, and present them with clarity. Go the extra mile in this. All young graduates drastically underestimate how much is going on in a manager's head. Sometimes you have to do the thinking for them. When given a task, do it, but also, when you can, go the extra mile.

6. Try to develop an interest outside work or your industry. Read widely around not just your own interests in perhaps sport, music or travel, but also business, economics, current affairs, psychology, etc. This not only helps with the all-important bonding you need to do with clients and colleagues but also develops your perspective on the world. Remember, you may be at work but you are still building relationships. Widening your knowledge makes you more rounded and more intelligent. It is transferable and will build your self-esteem.

7. Try to be strategic with your learning, for example, aim to master one skill and then move on to another. Use your journal, the first Key discussed, to master your discipline thoroughly by thinking analytically and to help with problem solving. Aim to become really good at least at one subject, process, practice or technology; something preferably that is in demand so that you don't lose track of the world around you.

Since your objective when you first start work is to develop work or soft skills, don't worry if your first or second job is not the job you dream about. For most people they rarely are. See your early working years as a training ground. If you are like most people, you will not work out what you are good at, or even what you want to become, until your late twenties or early thirties.

Some years ago, I coached a young graduate who seemed to me to be ideally suited for work in advertising, at a creative agency. After a couple of internships, she finally landed a job at one of London's leading agencies, only to be made redundant a few months later. They'd lost a large piece of business and she was one of the casualties. Naturally, she was disappointed. But, as she spoke to me, she began to look at the advantages and what she had gained. She now knew what it was like to work for a great agency; she knew who the other great agencies were, what she was good at, and what she wanted to do. She now found herself in stronger position to look for the job she really wanted.

It took me five years of working before I felt that advertising was the right job for me. In the first 18 months I loathed it. I wanted to work in the City, as it seemed to be the right sort of thing for me to do. I had made a decent fist of being a student rep at university, so I even considered becoming a Member of Parliament. And, at one point, my passion for music led me to apply for a marketing manager's role at a record company. It soon became apparent at the interview that it was an awful job. Music may have been my passion but I realised it wasn't the industry for me.

As I began to learn more about myself it became clearer to me what I liked to do best. I needed a job where my brain would be constantly stretched and stimulated, and that is what advertising did for me. Clients came in with problems and said, "Can you help us solve this?" and I loved this element.

I am not a great believer of the "follow your passion to find the job you're destined to do" sort of advice. You may not know it now but you will be a radically different person after five to ten years of working. You will have undergone a voyage of self-discovery. This may lead you to decide that today's ideal job may be far from ideal in the future. You may find you want to do something entirely different.

You can't work out what job will suit you until you have a full toolbox of work-related skills. Don't start your career by trying to find the 'soul mate' version of a job. Just get stuck in and then along the way you will discover what you are good at. That's when you can ask, "What aspects of the job do I like?", and then seek to transfer those skills into something else completely.

I have worked as an account manager, an account director, a managing director and then owned and run different companies but I have never had a more satisfying and fulfilling job than I do now, coaching people to develop a great career for themselves. However, I can spot the theme running through all the different jobs I have held. In all of them, I have always enjoyed developing people and bringing out the best in them, but I hardly knew how significant that was at the time.

So, allow time for your personality to develop, not only throughout your twenties and early thirties, but also beyond.

In the meantime, learn the skills you need to acquire to become successful in the workplace. For example, learn to work with people you don't particularly like; people who are much older than you; people who are introverts and people who are extroverts. Working in a company is all about collaboration, vastly different from university and school, where it's all about you. In short, learn all you can. If nothing else, it will build your self-esteem.

Exercise 3: Before all else, seek to learn

1. Take note of what happens in your organisation. What are other people working on right? Where are the big wins and priorities? Ask yourself: What have I learnt and how can I use it to help me do a better job?

2. Find out how your job and department fits in with the rest of the organisation.

3. Allow yourself time to learn about a new task before rushing into it. Get the facts first. And ask for help when you need it.

Chapter 4

The Fourth Key: You Learn Best from a Great Boss

A great boss challenges you in the right ways, leading but not managing. Gives you the room to stretch but supports you. when the going gets tough. A great boss is priceless.

Seth Godin

What's covered?

◆ The quickest way to learn is by watching others, particularly those who are brighter than you are.

◆ All great bosses are great learners, great communicators and great people developers.

◆ If your boss is failing, you will likely fail too, because you will learn nothing.

My next piece of advice is to try to find a great boss to work for. It took me some time to realise this, but the only type of boss you will learn from is a great one. In the first dozen years of my working life I had many different managers. I must have had ten or twelve in total. Three were great; one was fantastic. When I think back to these great bosses I realise that I learnt ten times more and ten times faster because they were so good.

I used to observe how one of these bosses, Geoff Howard-Spink, dealt with clients. He was a working class boy from the back streets of Battersea who had studied at Cambridge. He didn't suffer fools gladly but, more than that, it was the sheer force of his intellect that astounded. When he was pitching or presenting ideas to clients, it was an impressive spectacle. Each occasion was a master class in how to communicate.

Geoff was a stickler for data. He'd want to know the underlying numbers, what the strategic issues were. He'd want facts, not conjecture. You could never walk into his office and say "I think..." because he'd want to know why. It was essential to have facts that backed up what you were saying.

Geoff and another of my great bosses, David Clifford, taught me how to interrogate an issue to uncover what lay beneath. I learnt to think about a problem from as many different angles as possible. Bosses like these were always pushing me to dig deeper to discover essential facts that would yield a clear understanding of the problems facing a client's business.

Once I was in possession of the facts, my good bosses taught me how to present those facts in a logical manner. Before a client meeting, they'd ask me to prepare a short note identifying the main points to be discussed. This would force me to focus on key strategic developments and to write down clearly the key questions that needed to be answered.

After I had worked for three or four years, I had earned a modicum of negotiating power. I refused to work for bosses that were anything but good because I knew I would learn nothing from a bad boss. The difference between a good boss and bad boss is like the difference between night and day. A good boss lights up a world of possibilities; a bad boss darkens it.

So how do you tell a good boss from a bad one? Bad bosses far outnumber good ones. So the answer to the question is that old chestnut, you'll know one when you see one. Good bosses are quick on their feet, have good brains and are generous with their help. You will notice them because of the way they interact with clients and staff. Their behaviour and use of emotional intelligence sets them apart.

Often, I would leave a meeting with one of my great bosses, marvelling at the way they had solved a problem in a matter of minutes that had troubled the clients for weeks.

This is just one of the reasons it's a privilege to work for a great boss.

I want to end the advice contained in this Key by again referring to the work of Carol Dweck. In *Mindset*, she demonstrates that when bosses are controlling and abusive they jeopardise the growth of everyone around them. She attests that this type of boss has a fixed mindset; one that doesn't seek opportunities but instead is self-serving. Those whose boss suffers from this fixed mindset worry about being judged. Instead of growing and learning and thus moving a company forward, the boss creates an environment that stagnates the company and is unpleasant to work within.

Nothing grows in an environment like that, least of all an employee's confidence and abilities. Courage and innovation are thwarted.

By contrast, her research shows that bosses with a mindset open to growth make better decisions. They are themselves good learners. They are better negotiators. They notice and celebrate progress in their employees. They also provide more opportunities for career development in those that work for them.

Those are all reasons why working for a good boss is so important for your career. So, whatever you do, try to work for a good boss. You won't learn anything from the other kind.

Exercise 4: Learn from a great boss

1. First, identify the great boss you want to learn from. Choose someone consistent in the skills you admire. He/she doesn't have to directly manage you but ideally should be accessible to you at least some of the time.

2. Study what they do by noting, reflecting on and practicing the skills yourself.

3. Don't be afraid to ask the boss for tips on how to improve your skills.

Chapter 5
The Fifth Key: Work for the Best Company that You Can

The time you spend working for a great company is when you learn best

Peter Drucker

What's covered?

◆ The best companies know who they are and what they want. They create an *esprit de corps* that makes you want to do well.

◆ The best companies are meritocracies and promote based on ability and achievement.

◆ You will pick up on the transformational atmosphere in a great company and therefore grow much more quickly.

The first advertising agency I worked for, J. Walter Thompson, was the biggest in Britain. In theory, it was also the most successful. I learnt things there, but I learnt much more at my second agency, Collett, Dickenson and Pearce. In 1973, when CDP hired me, it was the best advertising agency in the world. It remained so for the next 10 years. People who had worked there were able to get jobs anywhere. To give you some idea of the sort of people who worked there, CDP's alumni include Sir Alan Parker, the film director, Lord Putnam, the film producer, and Charles Saatchi, mover and shaker in the art world.

But why was it that CDP was so good? And why was it that it was such a great place to work? Quite simply because everyone who worked there from the doorman to the chairman knew that the agency's sole purpose was to produce great creative work. Nothing else. CDP knew exactly what sort of people it wanted to hire, what sort of clients it wanted to work for, and what sort of work it wanted to do. Every piece of work the agency produced from the simplest trade ad to a huge television campaign had care and talent lavished upon it. Consequently, the esprit de corps was amazing. Everyone who worked there thought they could walk on water. And often it felt as if they did. It was wonderful to work in an environment like that.

In every industry there are a handful of companies that are the best, or striving to become the best. They aren't necessarily the biggest, but they excel at what they do, because their managements have a clear idea of what they are doing, how to go about doing it, and why they are doing it.

Great companies are always meritocracies. They do not promote on the basis of age or seniority, or for reasons of nepotism or political expediency. They promote people, and often at a fast speed, purely and simply because these people excel at what they do.

One last point: it's not the end of the world if you don't work at a great company in your first or second job. Great companies are harder to get into than average ones, not least because their bosses set high standards. Use your time at an average company to learn about your chosen industry. It will soon become clear which companies are the great ones. Once you know that, set about trying to get a job at one.

In *Talent is Overrated*, Geoffrey Colvin says that when most people are learning to do a job, they do so at a great speed. However, once they reach a reasonable level of competency they tend to plateau. They remain there, never getting better at what they do. Worse, they can even start to degenerate, as the work environment around them changes at a much faster pace than they are now developing. This is "so commonplace that we scarcely notice it, yet it's critically important to the success or failure of our organisations, the causes we believe in, and our own lives", Colvin says.

It's no different in any workplace. You won't get very far in your career working in a place that doesn't foster your progress. You will understand this fully if you go from working at an average company to a truly great one. You'll find the atmosphere intoxicating. If those working around you excel, you will strive to excel, too.

Exercise 5: Work for the best company you can

1. Find a company with the sort of reputation you want to be associated with, one that's the best in its field. What makes it great? Study its culture, mission and expertise.

2. What would help make you attractive to the company? What do you know? What skills do you have, or can you develop?

3. Work on those skills. Keep up to date with developments in your field and keep your LinkedIn profile page updated.

4. If the headhunter doesn't come to you, go to the head hunter. Email your CV to the recruiter that represents the organisation you want to work for with a cover letter explaining your career goals.

5. No luck? Don't give up. Keep working on your skills and knowledge, and stay in touch. Have an updated CV ready for when a vacancy arises.

Chapter 6

The Sixth Key: Learn to be Resilient

As much as talent counts, effort counts twice

Angela Duckworth

What's covered?

◆ Resilience is made up of the skills of perseverance and grit
– while perseverance takes you through the short term,
grit is for the long haul and takes you all the way.

◆ You'll need resilience for a whole variety of occasions, from
getting through tough times to acquiring a cognitively demanding skill.

◆ There will be days when you will cry, but that's normal.
Keep going.

Let us return to the late 1970s. I was working at CDP Aspect,
the London advertising agency that I had co-founded.

It was a near disaster. In our first year, we had pitched for 24
accounts, but had won only four.

I was a 27-year-old managing director, who looked more like
22, leading an untried team of people. No wonder we were
having trouble attracting clients.

Things became even tougher when our biggest client defected to another agency.

Then, to make matters worse my co-founder returned to the main agency, CDP. He thought CDP Aspect was doomed to failure.

I felt really down.

On top of that, every time we lost a presentation, I would telephone the client and ask why we hadn't been successful. But they only answered in platitudes.

It's similar to when a graduate asks for feedback about why he or she didn't get a job. People don't like to tell the truth because they think it might be hurtful, so they spin a meaningless line instead.

That was what was happening to us at CDP Aspect, time and time again.

I was in despair. I was on the verge of giving up. But, somehow, stubbornness and a sense of pride kept me going. This was my agency and I was determined to make it work.

Then, while I was on the telephone with yet another client whose business we'd failed to win, a flash of inspiration hit me. Instead of asking the usual single question about why we hadn't won I told him that I had five questions I would like him to answer.

He agreed, so I began to break down the individual parts of the presentation. I asked about the quality of the creative work, strategic thinking, the media plan, and so on. He said all were excellent.

I was confused. Other clients usually mumbled something about the creative work not being good enough, and left it at that.

Then I asked my final question: "Well, if you liked the work, liked the thinking, liked the media plan, why didn't you give us the business?"

I can remember his answer to this day.

"Chris," he said, "you talked too much in the presentation and, while we liked what you said, you had five other people in the room and you didn't allow them to get a word in edgeways. We need a team of people working on our business, not one man. What happens if you fall under a bus?"

It was my light bulb moment.

At last, a client had finally told me the truth.

I thanked him profusely and immediately began a radical overhaul of the way we pitched.

My resilience and perseverance had begun to pay off. I'd received feedback that told me how to change future pitches, the kind of feedback that, if I were to grow the business, I desperately needed.

You will need resilience in many different situations over the course of your working life, from persevering through difficult times, to developing a cognitively demanding skill, to developing that skill to a level of mastery.

The dictionary defines resilience as "the ability to recover speedily from problems". But I prefer the way that Angela Duckworth describes it, as 'grit'.

Angela and her research team at the University of Pennsylvania have given us greater understanding of the strategies that help a person learn how to work hard and adapt in the face of temptation, distraction, and defeat. How do high achievers keep going when the way is difficult? Angela's contention is that it's natural for human beings to feel frustrated, confused and challenged when trying to do something new. Ironically, she believes it to be a sure sign that we're getting somewhere.

Angela also clearly differentiates between grit and self-control, and explains that they are two completely different qualities. Self-control helps people resist giving in to short-term temptations. Grit, on the other hand, enables us to go the full distance and to achieve the breakthrough we crave.

Speaking about grit and self-control at a news conference in 2012, Angela described how these two aptitudes have featured in her own work. She described the many hours of meticulous testing and measuring, and then the need to do it all over again. She said it required diligence, and at times even drudgery. There will be times of uncertainty, of not knowing what you are doing, even after a couple decades. If it were not so, it would be a sign you had stopped learning. But grit will get you through.

Grit certainly got me through.

Now it was time to apply the feedback I'd been given. In my seven years at CDP I had taken part in quite a few pitches. When I reviewed these pitches in my head I remembered that they were minutely choreographed to make sure that everyone spoke.

Why hadn't I done the same thing?

It was because most of the people I pitched with were inexperienced in that kind of forum, which allowed me to dominate them. All our pitches to date had essentially been the Chris Davies show.

As I now knew, that wasn't what clients wanted.

So, I changed things. Our pitches at CDP Aspect were no longer the Chris Davies show. They were the CDP Aspect show, with all participants taking an active role. We began to win, and win big. Within two years, eight out of every ten clients we pitched to awarded us their business.

And, everything that I learnt from those years of successfully training others to pitch informs what I teach graduates today about getting jobs. After all, what is a job interview if it isn't a pitch?

The moral of this story is self-evident. Never, ever, give up.

As Angela's research shows, success rarely comes easily. More often than not it is the result of perspiration, not inspiration.

The one thing I had going for me was perspiration in the form of grit. I refused to give up.

Here, it's important to understand that this resilience wasn't worship to the god of hopeless causes. I had been told that our work was good and that our thinking was good. It was just that I had failed to realise the importance that clients attach to the need to work with a team, not an individual.

Our ideas were good but the way we were going about them was wrong.

Should you be faced one day with a similar situation – and there's every chance that you will – first make sure that what you are doing is right and, if you can reassure yourself that it is, carry on.

David Meketon, a research specialist on Angela's team, and a man who describes himself as "being in my third act", prepares new applicants who dream of working at the top-performing institution with this warning: "There will be days when you will cry. That's normal. Just keep going."

As long as you remember these words, it will come good. Eventually.

Exercise 6: Learn to be resilient

1. Select a 'hard thing' to commit to. Write it down keeping in mind that learning is about trial and error.

2. It's been said that life is 10 per cent of what happens to you and 90 per cent of how you react to it. Whenever you want to give up, tell yourself, "I have the greater control, which is control over my attitude".

3. Prepare your mind ahead. Remind yourself that setbacks, struggles and even boredom are normal parts of growth and discovering new things.

4. Allow time for resilience to develop.

Chapter 7

The Seventh Key: Build Networks and Make Friends

The time to build a network is always before you need one.

Douglas Conant

What's covered?

◆ You need to build and develop meaningful reciprocal networks with people who you get to know.

◆ People with strong social networks are more likely to do well at work and in life.

◆ Make networks with people at all levels of your company and industry, and also outside of the industry, because you never know when a person will come in handy.

It might surprise you to learn that most people underestimate the importance of building networks and making friends. I have worked with people who used to guard jealously the projects they were working on. I have always been exactly the opposite. I would never divulge a confidence but I would always be open and say things like "this is what's going on with the business I handle, what happening with yours?" Or simply, "how are you, how are you getting on?" I would always try to be generous with my time and help others if I could.

Today, if I talk to a young person about building networks, the first thing that comes into their mind is social media. While that's good, it's not the sort of network I am talking about. I am talking about a quality network, one that really means something to you. It means mixing with real people in real time. It means getting to know those people well.

It's essential that your network includes people from different levels within your industry and within your organisation. For one thing, it will probably make working life easier and more pleasant. For another, and perhaps more importantly, it's because you never know when these contacts might come in handy. So nurture them.

It is also wise to seek members of your network from outside your industry. I always maintained a circle of friends outside advertising. Conversations with these networkers can become the source of insights and knowledge that would otherwise have been denied you. You will be able to make connections between what, on the face of them, are totally unrelated items of information, and what you learn from this process will favourably set you apart from your co-workers and others.

Strong networks provide access to information, support and advice that help to build your career. My bosses were often startled by some of the things I discovered.

I first came to realise the power of a network at CDP. Once I started at the company, I realised immediately that it was a much friendlier place than J. Walter Thompson; one where I hoped I could start to thrive. However, like all organisations it was a very competitive environment.

I was determined to learn as much as possible as quickly as I could. However, everyone at my level used to guard their knowledge carefully, revealing little to their work colleagues about what they were learning. Information is power, after all.

So, how could I learn not just about the accounts that I was working on but every other account? There was of course no internet or intranets in those days; everything was written down in documents. The best documents to read were the annual brand and advertising plans. These used to contain everything you needed to know about a client's business; the idea being that if someone left or was ill a new person could immediately be drafted on to an account and get up to speed quickly.

So, once I had realised that, I knew that if I wanted to learn how the entire agency worked quickly then I would need to try and persuade my colleagues to let me read their brand plans at weekends.

Only one problem: why should someone give up their precious secrets?

Everyone had their own little office in those days. Mine was on a floor with about twenty other people on it. I was the account manager on Birds Eye frozen foods. Surprisingly, I soon discovered that our client in their infinite wisdom had decided that we advertising folk should have access to all their food so that we could appreciate how good it was. So, we had our own store account and Birds Eye lorries used to deliver whatever had been ordered, just like a normal retail store. The good news for me was that I was in charge of the weekly order, and I soon discovered nobody cared how much I ordered. So, after a month of feeding my flatmates on burgers, cheesecakes, Arctic rolls and numerous culinary delights, I decided that what I should do was to expand my largesse to include all twenty of my work colleagues.

However, they had to agree that, in return for free frozen cheesecakes, burgers or whatever else, they had to swap me a precious brand plan so that I could read it over the weekend. It worked. I soon became the most popular man on my floor and the most knowledgeable too! Every Friday afternoon I would do the Birds Eye run and exchange food for documents.

After a couple months or so I had read everything but, rather than just withdrawing the free food offer, I decided just to keep handing it out anyway. As a result, I started to make friends quickly, and some of those friendships stood me in very good stead years later, as I was to discover.

The creative guys also started to hear about this and so I started supplying them as well, which came in very useful when I needed a favour.

Little did I know that at the tender age of 23 I had discovered the power of a network.

In his book, *The Happiness Advantage*, Shawn Achor writes about this in a Massachusetts Institute of Technology (MIT) study conducted for IBM. The study involved MIT researchers spending an entire year following 2,600 employees, observing their social ties, even using mathematical formulae to analyse the size and shape of their address books.

They found that the more socially connected they were the better they performed. They could even quantify the difference: on average, every email contact was worth an additional $948 in revenue.

So impressed were IBM with the results of this research that they started a programme to facilitate the introductions of employees who didn't yet know each other and also taught everyone how to make contacts with people in other firms.

Achor's principle for how to achieve happiness by finding success and performance at work is called 'social investment'. He says social support is your single greatest asset.

This certainly proved to be the case for me in an event that was far more challenging than the Birds Eye scenario. Let me explain.

At Collett, Dickenson and Pearce I made the effort to be friendly with as many people as possible. This paid off handsomely when I wanted to undertake a management buyout of CDP Aspect. I'd had problems building the business because on many occasions a bank, say, would refuse to allow us to pitch when they discovered that the main agency, CDP, handled one of their rivals. However, the top bosses of CDP were opposed to a buyout. CDP's chief executive convened a board meeting at which he gave his reasons for not allowing a buyout to go ahead. But many board members were also members of my network. They were friends. They urged the chief executive to allow me to move ahead. They could see that CDP Aspect would never grow while shackled to CDP. So my management buyout went ahead. That's just one practical example of the value of a network. Here's another.

It concerns the early days of a new way of analysing demographic groups based on what they bought and where they lived, rather than what job they did. It was called 'A Classification of Residential Neighbourhoods', or ACORN, for short.

This new way of looking at people's demographics and behaviour was revolutionary. The inventors were casting around for clients to sign up to it. I thought it was a clever way of understanding who bought your product and why. I could see its uses as a new business tool for my agency. And, because the ACORN people were friends of mine I was able to go and make them an offer. I said that if they did a special analysis for me without charge, on the basis that if I won the account I was pitching for, I would make sure that ACORN got analytical work from that client. I was able to go into pitches armed with free data about the client and his brand that ACORN had given me, data that no other agency in town had access to. It was a pitch-winning tool, and all down to the fact that my network had included the people who invented ACORN.

So, always try to be nice to people. Always try to be generous with your time. That doesn't mean letting someone walk all over you, nor take advantage of your niceness. Make friends. Keep friendly with them. Despite what is sometimes said, nice people do finish first.

Exercise 7: Build networks

1. If you haven't already done so, set up a professional LinkedIn profile and start joining relevant groups. Don't limit yourself to online networks only – network at live events too.

2. Build your own useful set of skills and knowledge. Become a person worth knowing.

3. Network with people in and outside of the company you work for. Don't forget those above, and those below... they may rise one day.

4. Get to know your contacts, and keep in touch.

Chapter 8

The Eighth Key: Ask for Projects Outside Your Comfort Zone

Move out of your comfort zone. You can only grow if you are willing to feel awkward and uncomfortable when you try something new.

Brian Tracy

What's covered?

1. To achieve mastery of a skill you must move to a place of advanced learning.

2. This demands experiences that force you to get out of your comfort zone.

3. Your brain will help you learn and become proficient at even the most cognitively demanding task by growing new connections and you don't have to wait 10,000 hours before you begin to see improvement!

Angela Duckworth, author of *Grit: The Power of Passion and Perseverance*, has a principle in her household called 'the hard thing rule'. Angela and her husband, Jason, use the hard thing rule as a way of familiarising their two young daughters with the experience of developing grit.

The hard thing rule requires that each family member always has a hard thing to learn in their lives. This could be acquiring new dance skills, playing a musical instrument or solving a problem at school or work. The hard thing rule is a way to advance their learning to a new level. It helps them practise and develop grit. They must practise at the hard thing daily and commit to it for an agreed period; and they must not quit in the middle just because it's difficult or boring.

Setting yourself a hard thing rule like this in your own life will ensure that your brain is constantly developing new connections. It ensures that you are constantly improving, which means constantly moving beyond your comfort level.

During the first year of starting to work, you'll just want to find your feet. That's absolutely right, but as soon as you can – and the sooner the better – you should begin to ask for projects that you don't really know a lot about. It is only when you move out of your comfort zone that you really learn.

Now let me tell you about Nigeria. A German Brewer was setting up a plant in Nigeria and needed some ads to run in that country. An English design company had created the brewer's labels and branding. The design company recommended Collett, Dickenson and Pearce to do the advertising. First and foremost, this project called for a trip to Nigeria. None of my fellow account managers wanted to go but I put myself forward, not least because the trip offered me the chance to travel and work closely with one of the directors who ran CDP. I soon found myself dealing directly with the top people from the German brewers, who were building the £50 million brewery in the jungle. I was also introduced to the Nigerian chief who was involved in the project, another person with whom I would be working – and, at the time – I was only 25 years old.

I was on a steep learning curve and it became even steeper a few days into the project. One of the Nigerian clients asked how much the advertising was going to cost. In those days, advertising agencies were paid 15 per cent commission on media billing. But the ads were to appear on Nigerian TV. We had no way of finding out what these costs might be. We had no alternative but to charge a fee, and I had to work it out right there, on the spot. I told them the figure and they said, "Yes, that's fine. Can you provide a breakdown of the fee?"

Neither my boss nor I had ever put together such a document. We had to create that document on a manual typewriter. We broke the project down into 25 different stages, put a cost against each one, with the number of man hours and people working on each stage. We delivered it the following morning.

So, here I was, this white guy from England, in the middle of the jungle, less than six months after the end of the Biafran war, totally outside of my comfort zone and having to learn with every new encounter. It was bizarre but exhilarating.

Now, some really heavy nonsense began when they said they could only pay us in the local currency, Naira. Nobody was allowed to take Naira out of the country so it was useless to us. We decided to see one of the Germans. We said, "You knew about this and it's no good to us". "Okay," he said, "what do you want?" We told him we wanted pounds sterling. "Well," he said, "we could do with the Naira to pay our local workers." So he took the Naira off our hands and gave us sterling in return.

After going through this experience, I wasn't afraid of anything ever again. It's true what they say. What doesn't kill you makes you stronger. And I returned from this trip stronger than ever before. A few years later this helped when I was asked to start CDP Aspect. I had no experience of starting an advertising agency but I didn't blink at the challenge. The Nigerian project also came to my aid when I proposed the management buyout of CDP Aspect. It helped my determination in the face of opposition from the chief executive of CDP.

So what does all this mean? By always welcoming projects, tasks and opportunities that sit outside your comfort zone you will grow stronger. You will more quickly acquire the confidence, skill and know-how needed in order to succeed.

I find that it helps to understand what's happening inside our brains when we take on new challenges like these. This is where we venture into the science of neuroplasticity again. Neuroplasticity helps us to understand how the brain works with our thoughts to change its own structure and function in response to mental experience. So, by exposing myself to this mental experience, I was effectively rewiring my brain to create totally new connections that did not exist before.

Psychologist Norman Doidge, author of *The Brain that Changes Itself*, states that neurons that fire together wire together. This means that repeated mental experience leads to structural changes in the brain's neurons that process that experience. The synaptic connections between these neurons then grow stronger. So, the more you do something the better you get at it. Your neurons are firing off stronger, deeper, faster signals and the circuit is becoming more efficient. But the opposite is also true: when you stop performing an action, these connections become weaker. It's a 'use it or lose it' phenomenon.

What does this mean for us? By continuously welcoming projects, tasks and opportunities outside your comfort zone you will grow stronger, faster. You will build the confidence, skills, know-how and expertise you need to succeed in your career. You will rewire your brain and grow as a person. And it will always be worth it.

We also now know that the process of growing new neural connections requires the dendrites to build up 'myelin sheaths'. This thin layer of covering grows over the nerves enabling them to send signals back and forth much more quickly.

Think about what happens when you are learning a new skill. At first, you probably perform it clumsily, but over time you become more proficient and quicker at it. Learning a skill takes time because the connecting of neurons and the process of myelination takes time.

This is especially true of the types of cognitively demanding tasks that you will be expected to master during your working life. They take you out of your comfort zone and the result is growth. You get better.

I experienced this most recently when learning to Tango. I've always considered myself to have two left feet so for me learning to dance is a miracle in itself. Even after a few years of learning, I still found it difficult to coordinate my feet correctly to perform a certain complicated move. But after continuous practice I eventually got it, and I didn't even notice until I realised I was actually doing it.

As Geoff Colvin says, "Experts are not born but made". Don't worry that it's uncomfortable. Remember, neurons are firing, wiring and connecting inside your brain. Once the connecting neurons are myelinated you will be able to master that new and once complex skill. And the great thing about it is that you don't have to wait the 10,000 hours researchers say it takes to master a skill before you begin to see some improvement. Keep at it and, just like my Tango, your progress will become increasingly better along the way.

Exercise 8: Ask for projects outside your comfort zone

1. Use the Praxis chart to help you to choose a new learning goal outside your area of comfort.

2. On a sheet of paper, draw a square and divide it into four equal box sections.

Familiar task in a familiar environment	Familiar task in an unfamiliar environment
Unfamiliar task in an unfamiliar environment	Unfamiliar task in a familiar environment

In the top left section write 'Familiar task in a familiar environment'. In the bottom left section below write, 'Unfamiliar task in an unfamiliar environment'. (These tasks are either inside your comfort zone OR well beyond it.)

3. In the top right section write 'Familiar task in an unfamiliar environment' and in the bottom right, 'Unfamiliar task in a familiar environment'. (These tasks will sit on the spectrum range between those that are in and those that are outside of your current comfort zone.)

4. Use the chart to list and choose projects to ask for outside of your comfort zone.

Chapter 9
The Ninth Key: Always Be Aware of the Numbers

The best business decisions are always based on the numbers

Warren Buffett

What's covered?

◆ Every organisation has an underlying set of numbers that you need to know. Never lose sight of them.

◆ These numbers will tell you how the organisation makes its money, how it works and what makes it successful.

◆ The numbers aren't necessarily 'numerical': they are simply the data that reveals the key performance indicators for your organisation and industry.

Most people don't try to understand how the company they work for earns money and therefore where the profits come from. The decisions that these people make are not governed by an understanding of key numbers. Let me give you an example of how I learned that numbers are important.

I am harking back to my time at Collett, Dickenson and Pearce again. One of the agency's clients was Fine Fare (now part of Morrisons), a supermarket chain. They were in direct competition with Tesco. Fine Fare discovered that Tesco were about to abandon Green Shield Stamps, so-called trading stamps that were given to customers as a reward when they shopped at Tesco. The stamps could be redeemed for gifts when enough had been collected. Abandoning Green Shield Stamps meant that Tesco were able to save money and pass this on to their customers in the form of lower prices. Fine Fare came to CDP and asked what they should do to respond. They said they would return in three weeks to hear how we thought Fine Fare should react. We spent the three weeks changing the Fine Fare ads we had, and creating new ones.

When Fine Fare's board returned, we proudly presented the advertisements that the agency had been working on. "Interesting," they said. "That's what we thought you might do. Shame you didn't ask us for the numbers."

There was a growing panic in the room amongst the agency members.

Fine Fare's commercial director said, "As you know we have 1,450 stores and Tesco have 1,850."

We nodded agreement.

"But do you know how many stores are within a three-mile radius and therefore trade directly against Tesco?"

We admitted that we didn't.

The commercial director continued. "If you'd have asked us we would have told you that there are only 74, so actually Tesco dropping their prices will only have an impact on 74 of our 1,450 stores. So why are you and your ads saying we should drop our prices in all our stores, and lose all that profit? Surely you can see that's a silly thing to say?"

They gave us a document showing all the stores that were trading against Tesco.

"This is what's going to happen," said the commercial director. "You are going to run ads for these stores in local papers that are relevant to these stores saying that our prices are 10 per cent cheaper than Tesco. But, in the other 1,376 stores we are going to do precisely nothing. Now we'll leave you, but we'll be back next week. Make sure you know your numbers before you talk to us then."

The meeting had lasted just over half an hour. You could have heard a pin drop in the room after they left. No one wanted to say anything, least of all my boss. It was the first time he'd been caught out like this. In all likelihood, it was the single most embarrassing moment in CDP's entire history, and all down to an elementary question that nobody had thought to ask: how many Fine Fare stores is this likely to affect?

When it came to it, Tesco did a first rate job of promoting their lower prices. Despite this, Fine Fare's market share did not suffer one iota. All the other supermarket chains panicked. They cut their prices and considerably lessened their profits.

After that, I was in no doubt as to the power and importance of numbers. You see, nobody can argue with numbers; they are facts, expressed as figures. Not conjecture, not gut feeling, not guesswork. But facts, hard facts.

The numbers give you the detail, and the detail gives you clearer sight of the big picture. You never want to lose the big picture.

Keeping sight of the numbers can therefore also be translated as keeping sight of the details. They don't have to be financial. For example, a good habit to practise when pitching or delivering any piece of work on behalf of a client is to reread the brief. Even if you think you know what they're asking, read it again. This will reduce the chance of you missing something crucial. It is also about understanding the key performance indicators in your company and industry – what makes it successful, or not. If you are working for a charity or in the public sector, there will still be a set of underlying numbers – key donors, statistics about the users, the most profitable fundraising activities and regions, and so forth.

A lot of this comes down to what's known as the 'Pareto' principle. This states that for many events, 80 per cent of the effects come down to 20 per cent of the causes. British Airways is a good example. Most of the profit the airline makes comes from 20 per cent of the seats they sell, premium seats like first class, and largely on trans-Atlantic routes. Every database I've looked at tells the same story. There are always a small number of small clients that are hugely important to the profitability of a company. It was certainly true of CDP. One client was responsible for generating 70 per cent of the agency's profit.

Once you have a firm grasp of how a company makes money, or what an organisation's key numbers are, you will be able to engage in much more meaningful debate and are unlikely to be embarrassed as we were that day with Fine Fare.

Exercise 9: Always be aware of the numbers

How many of the following numbers do you know about the place where you work?

◆ Fastest moving products/services

◆ Most often requested products or services

◆ Most asked customer question or complaint

◆ Longest running service

◆ Top 20 per cent of customers that spend the most

◆ Bottom 20 per cent of customers spending the least

◆ How many people visit your company site?

◆ How many enquiries do you get through?

◆ How many buy or order something?

◆ How many become repeat purchasers?

Chapter 10
The Tenth Key: Always Deliver More than Expected

All successful employers are stalking men who will do the unusual, men who think, men who attract attention by performing more than is expected of them.

Charles M. Schwab

What's covered?

◆ Doing what you are paid to do is nothing special, so go over and above what you are paid to do.

◆ Whatever you do, be a problem solver and someone who adds value wherever you go.

◆ Introducing the element of surprise helps the brain to break up the predictable and gets your work noticed.

Always strive to deliver more than expected, and deliver on time. You are being paid for your work, so if you do a good job that's okay. But that's the point. It's just okay. So, instead of delivering only what you've been asked for, deliver extra. Say to your boss or your client, "Here's what you asked for, but how about this? And this? And this?"

The time I learnt this was when I was working with a small client, Myers Beds. We made only one TV commercial a year for Myers, but we seemed to spend all year talking about it. It was boring.

I tried to discuss the situation with my boss but he didn't appear interested. It later occurred to me that small accounts such as Myers were how the agency let relatively inexperienced account handlers cut their teeth. If they got something wrong it wouldn't do too much harm as it might on a large piece of business. Anyway, we decided to look at the Myers bed range in the stores of London's Oxford Street. It soon became apparent that Slumberland beds were always displayed in a more prominent position than Myers' were.

Slumberland also seemed to charge a premium. They cost £100 more than Myers' beds. A store manager explained that Slumberland covers were more attractive than those on Myers' beds. Strangely, people buy on appearance, despite the fact that the bed spends its life covered up. Slumberland's better-designed covers allowed it to charge more.

It all made sense. One of my friends worked on a whisky account whose packaging was a step above the norm. He told me that they too could charge a higher price than their competitors. So I came up with an idea.

Another of the accounts I handled was Mary Quant, the cosmetic and fashion brand. I asked Mary Quant to design a range of covers for Myers. That led to Myers being able to charge £100 more for their special Mary Quant range of covers. And what do you think the cost of these new covers was? £2. Boy, did this transform Myers's attitude towards us at the agency. Suddenly we changed from mere suppliers of advertising to business partners. We never had any problems or tedious meetings with commercials after that.

Of course, there is sometimes a risk with these things. If you are asked to deliver a certain outcome by a client or a boss, how do you go over and above without upsetting the client or veering too far from the brief?

Here's what I learned about the right and wrong way to tell a client, your boss, a customer or whoever, that you think your ideas are better than theirs.

When we were first starting out at CDP Aspect, we took part in some filming for a reality TV show. A number of agencies were asked to present ideas for an advertising campaign to the client, who would choose the winning pitch at the end. The client asked for a general advertising campaign for all of their products but we thought their campaign would be so much stronger with a focus on their key product, which was television sets. But they did not like our ideas and after the first three episodes we were off the show. We had wasted a huge opportunity to promote ourselves on national TV.

I learnt later that the way to approach a situation like this is to present exactly what the client wants and then to say, "We've also thought about this and that. What do you think?" That way, you're happy because you've presented what you be-lieve will really work, and the client is happy because you've presented what he asked for. It's then left up to the client to decide which option he'd like to go with. Even if he doesn't take up your ideas, it doesn't matter; at least you know you've put them forward. It is only by taking the risk to beyond and above what everyone else is doing that you can stand out, break out of the norm and set new trends.

Doing the unexpected not only works but is necessary, says Andy Nulman, author of *POW! Right Between the Eyes*. His book explores the idea of using the power of surprise in busi-ness as a way of going over and above what people normally expect. Andy states that the element of surprise is more im-portant today than ever before because people are bom-barded with so much information from so many different sources that they just 'zone out'. Most of this information is standardised and boring – just like those adverts were for the bed company.

You'll find this trend everywhere. Most people perform their jobs in the same standardised way as the man or woman sitting beside them. Seth Godin, a true maestro of modern marketing, says, "If you expect me to take action I've never taken before, it seems to me that you need to do something that hasn't been done before." That's what gets people talking about you. That's what makes you memorable. And that's what we did with Myers Beds.

Surprise, says Andy, is what differentiates us. It's the difference between a "Holy jeez!" and a "Who cares?" And it doesn't matter whether you are selling products, political messages or yourself. When you give someone something they did not expect, you are more likely to make an impact that both gets results and lasts.

I recently learned that there is a scientific way to look at this. During an interview with Ray Dolan FRS, professor of neuropsychiatry at UCL, ex-Guardian editor, Alan Rusbridger, asked why it was that certain musicians, although they can play well, find it difficult or nearly impossible to invoke any sense of emotion in their music. Alan had recently met the pianist Angela Hewitt, who told him about her experience of teaching music to children in China. She said that although they could play note perfect and had trained since they were very young, their playing was bereft of emotion.

Ray explained that this is because our brains predict sensory input about what we should expect. Those predictions reduce the processing demands on the brain; it's the brain's way of being efficiently resourceful. He told Alan that in this zone, "You're making predictions of the consequences of your actions. And those predictions, they perfectly line up with the consequences so you don't notice anything. It's only when there's a deviation that you notice. And that deviation in mathematical terms is called 'surprise'.

And there you have it. Surprise is scientifically proven to work.

Exercise 10: Deliver more than expected

1. Small steps add up, so think about how can you improve the quality of the service you offer, even if just a fraction.

2. Keep within the parameters of what's expected of you – there's no point going over and above in an area that's not a priority for your boss or the organisation as a whole. Work on adding value to the right things and in the right areas.

Chapter 11
The Eleventh Key: Be Authentic

People are always judging you based on where you're from, where you went to school, how you look, how you talk. But at the end of the day, you're going to have to look into the mirror and accept who you are. It's all about being authentic.

Andre Carson

What's covered?

◆ Be yourself. It's far too draining to try to be what you are not.

◆ Emulate others, but take what you admire from them and express it in your own unique way.

◆ It takes all sorts to build a successful team – the introvert and the extrovert each have their role to play.

One of my coaching clients recently landed her first job. After a few weeks she came to me. "I don't think I'm fitting in," she said. "Everyone else is close-knit but I'm not like them. We go out for drinks after work and I'm nervous and introverted."

I told her not to worry, not everyone can be an extrovert. Just be yourself.

I understood her feelings. Once, early in my career, I tried to rid myself of my Geordie accent. I wanted to sound like everyone else around me. I soon realised it was pointless. Nobody should ever try to change who they are.

The hard truth is that it takes all sorts to make any organisation work. Bosses like to build teams whose members have complementary talents. That's how teams work best, when they are made up of different types of people.

V. S. Naipaul once said that a person isn't born as themselves but "with a mass of expectations, a mass of other people's ideas and you have to work through it all". There is a lot of advice being shared about 'who' you need to be in order to be successful but the best thing you can do is become the best version of yourself that you possibly can. That should be your aim. Build your own self-esteem. Build yourself.

Authenticity matters, and trying to become something else can make one feel schizophrenic. You will not come across as genuine. Sure, mimic others for the traits you admire in them, but then take those traits and express them in your own authentic way. For example, if you wanted to become a talk show host like Oprah you wouldn't want to do it exactly the same way she does but adopt the skills and methods she employs to your own situation.

Take the example of speaking or presenting before an audience. Many people find this scary but the worst thing they can do is to go out on stage and pretend to be someone else. There are, of course, factors that make for a great presentation, and your task is to adopt these and express them in a way that is authentic to you.

Let me give you a personal example about why you should learn to be yourself.

There was a time when I decided to learn more about how to give a speech. By then, I was already an accomplished presenter, having regularly to present ideas to clients. But I hadn't realised the essential differences between speeches and presentations, of which there are many. So, after having bombed completely in my first speech, which was to my ad agency peers, I realised that I had to have some coaching.

I chose an ex-actress who had just started working as coach. I took her in specifically to help me with a big speech that I was to give to 3,000 people at their company's annual sales conference. I was to present our advertisements for our newest client. It was a big day.

I was told by my new teacher that when you are on stage with that many people in the audience you should speak slowly. I duly did so. And... I was a disaster and had to be pulled off stage.

I had totally misread my audience but, even more importantly, I had totally failed to get my personality across, which is positive, upbeat and energetic. I hadn't been true to myself.

I was in despair and decided to look around the bookshops for a book. One of the advantages of good, old-fashioned bookshops is that you can browse the books first, which I did. One book caught my eye: *Leading Out Loud*. The author wisely said that, apart from the importance of rehearsing in front of a mirror – an hour for each five minutes of a speech – you need to be true to yourself. Whether you're speaking in public to five or 5,000 people, it doesn't matter.

So, if you're no good at telling jokes, don't attempt to. If your natural speaking manner is fast and furious, be fast and furious. If you are relaxed, be relaxed. Just don't attempt to be something you are not. Ever!

After that horrible day, I never looked back. I started striding round stages talking nineteen to the dozen and even going down the aisle closer to the audience. Eventually, I even learnt to speak using the bare minimum of notes – all because I trusted myself to be myself! My advice, therefore, is don't let anyone ever persuade you to be something you are not.

To thine own self be true... always!

To illustrate this, let's return to introverts. Susan Cain, a former lawyer and accomplished negotiations consultant, says that being sociable and outgoing is often prized over being quiet and contemplative. But we need people of both types. Most workplaces are open plan, and thus designed for extroverts. The idea, of course, is to encourage collaborative teamwork. But it's possible to make a meaningful contribution, even if you are introverted. Businesses and organisations require both the man or woman of action and the man or woman of contemplation.

"Our offices should be encouraging casual, chatty, café-style interaction where people come together and serendipitously come up with new ideas," says Cain "but we also need privacy, autonomy and ability to work alone."

I was good at building relationships, so people often mistook me for a social animal. In truth, I rarely attended social events outside of working hours. I spent that time with my family. However, in no way did this prevent me from building professional networks, connections and friendships. I just did it my way.

This is what makes a strengths-based approach to professional development so interesting. In *Now, Discover Your Strengths*, Marcus Buckingham and Donald Clifton encourage us to discover our strengths, develop them, then use them to complement the strengths of other people who are different from us. It's all about making the most of your difference. Even people who appear to have the same type of strength often exhibit small differences and the strengths-based approach recognises this. Take relationship building, for example. One person might be great at starting relationships; another might be better at sustaining them. Imagine the effect these two could have if they identified and valued these differences, and then fused them to work together.

Once I'd worked this out for myself I was better able to match different team personalities with different clients. Team members were then capable of bringing their unique perspectives and skills to bear. When all members of a team are the same, their employer is disadvantaged. So don't try to be like those around you. Be yourself.

Celebrate your difference from others and value it. Bear this in mind whenever you feel that you don't fit in. Remember it when you feel different. Don't try to change yourself. Don't try to become someone you're not. Pretending to be somebody else takes too much time and effort anyway. Just be you.

Exercise 11: Be authentic

1. Accept who you are. Identify the skills that are unique to you and own them. Work on them, develop them, talk about them and champion them.

2. If you've never done one before, take a personality test to help you to learn more about your dominant character traits. Begin with the free ones available online.

Chapter 12

The Twelfth Key: Find a Mentor or Coach

Listen to advice from people who have been there and done that. It is so hard to believe that when you are young, but parents, mentors, teachers, they can all be so valuable when it comes to advice.

Lauren Conrad

What's covered?

◆ You will need a mentor or a coach if you are to become above average at what you do.

◆ Your mentor or coach should be someone with the years of experience and wisdom needed to help you accelerate your learning.

◆ Your mentor or coach should be someone who believes in you and is honest enough to tell you what they really think.

If you want to improve your skills, you must find a mentor or coach. Throughout my career I have always worked with people who mentored one another. Today, I still mentor an old work colleague who's become a good friend, Jeff Fugler. Jeff still mentors me. He's my go-to guy if I have a problem to discuss. I can say something like, "I am thinking of doing such-and-such to sort this out. What do you think?" We've both been in business for more years than we care to remember. Over those years we've learnt much. So we are able to provide each other with insightful advice.

In the early days of your career your mentor should be older than you, or at least have more experience. It also helps if they see things from a slightly different perspective. It's important, too, that your mentor is non-judgmental, so don't fall back on a parent or relation to fulfil this role. Find someone who can remain independent from friends and family if possible.

So what's different about a coach? A coach has usually done what you wish to do. A coach will draw on his or her experience to help you attain a specific goal. That's what I do; help people achieve their career ambitions.

However, it doesn't really matter whether you call the person a mentor or a coach. The two terms are often used interchangeably, anyway, and can draw on the same set of skills. It just matters that you find someone who can help you move forward in your career.

Having a mentor or coach is essential if you wish to become excellent at what you do, says Anders Ericsson. You will need either or both at some point in your working life if you are to become above average. If you look at anyone who is accomplished to a standard of excellence in any skill – be they musician, writer, sportsperson or business professional – you will find that at some point they had the benefit of a great teacher, coach or mentor. For example, Sir Alan Parker, the film director mentioned earlier in this book had fellow director, Fred Zimmerman, as his mentor.

Ericsson explains that by giving constructive feedback, learning becomes quicker. A coach can suggest fast lanes to take and pitfalls to avoid. Often their advice might be painful to hear but it will prove vital for anyone who is serious about perfecting their craft or skill. If you are about to do something disastrous, isn't it better to have someone who's honest enough to tell you, rather than keep quiet? Or nobody at all? Of course, it is. A further advantage that a coach offers is recognition of what learning stage you've reached. A coach will know what you can manage now, and what should be dealt with later. He or she will encourage you to work on the right areas at the right time.

A good place to start to find a mentor or a coach is by looking at those who have influenced and inspired you in your life. Look first among the people you admire and who have helped you along the way. Look at your teachers, lecturers, work experience bosses. Look among the networks you are building. Don't overlook the industry specialists that come to do talks at career fairs, industry events and conferences. Just ask. You never know until you do.

There are certain characteristics that have been identified as desirable attributes to look out for in a good mentor. Daniel Coyle in his book, *The Little Book of Talent: 52 tips for improving your skills*, says that you should:

1. Avoid someone who is too nice to you. He calls it the 'courteous waiter syndrome'. While this is nice to have in a waiter, it's not quite what you want from a coach or mentor.

2. Seek someone who scares you a little; someone you respect highly. This is a person who is observant, good at figuring people out, action-orientated and honest, even if brutally so.

3. Seek someone who gives short, clear directions. You don't want someone who waffles or is long-winded, but someone who is straight-to-the-point and tells you exactly what you need to know.

4. Seek someone who loves teaching the fundamentals. Daniel describes this as a person who breaks things down and clearly explains the small but key or important parts

of the whole so that you fully understand how it all fits together.

5. Try to find someone older than yourself. This is because the greatest teachers are first learners, and learning improves with time. A wise old hat will have seen a few things.

Your mentor should also be someone who knows about making mistakes and bouncing back from them. They have grit, or perseverance, as a result of overcoming obstacles in order to pursue a passion in their own lives. In a study by Teach America, published in the *Journal of Positive Psychology*, researchers assessed the success of 390 teachers one year before and after teaching. They found that those who scored high for grit were 31 per cent more likely to inspire academic growth in their students. Somehow, the sense of overcoming setbacks, staying on track and remaining focused on their life goals provided invaluable insights that inspired students to do the same.

One other thing: a great mentor is someone who believes in you; they have high expectations of you. High expectation was first discovered to play a significant role in student learning outcome in a study carried out by Rosenthal and Jacobson as part of the 'No Child Left Behind' federal legislation in America. At the time, the concept of low and high expectations was dismissed as having no bearing on a child's ability to do well until the book *Pygmalion in the Classroom* forced a change of mind.

The book reported the outcome of an exercise in which teachers were told that some of the students in their classes were 'academic sputters' – students who had been given a test that identified not only high IQs but also the capability of making rapid, above average, intellectual progress in the coming year. In fact, the children were singled out randomly. They weren't sputters at all.

However, because the teachers' expectations were high and they expected the students to do well, they did. In fact, 30 per cent of these children increased by an average of 22 IQ points and almost all gained an additional 10 IQ points. It wasn't that the teachers spent more time with these students but that they were more enthusiastic about teaching them. The research authors concluded that a self-fulfilling prophecy was at work.

So, you need someone who is rooting for you, someone you can discuss work problems with. Ideally, this should not be your boss. He or she will be too busy, anyway. But somebody who works outside the company you work for, somebody who is a good listener and has the experience to be able to offer good advice. They won't always have all the answers, but they should possess the necessary wisdom to help you work out most things out for yourself.

However, there may come a time when you outgrow your coach or mentor. It's important to recognise when it happens, as this can also stunt your progress. For this reason, you may need different mentors at different times in your career.

Exercise 12: Find a mentor or coach

1. Look at current and past course leaders and managers where you've studied, worked, or volunteered. Consider people in your network.

2. Approach them by email explaining that you would like for them to become your coach or mentor. Share your goals with them and tell them why you're approaching them. For example, you admire their public speaking abilities and would love the opportunity to learn from them.

Chapter 13

The Thirteenth Key: Adopt a 'Can-Do' Attitude

No matter what the recipe, any baker can do wonders in the kitchen with some good ingredients and an upbeat attitude!

Buddy Valastro

What's covered?

◆ Be the person who says, "I'll find a way" and you will inspire your boss to entrust more to you.

◆ Positive people are more likely to perform better at life and work on every level.

◆ There is a solution to every problem, and often, if you give it time, the right one will present itself.

When the boss or client asks "Can you do this?" make sure you're the person who says, "Yes I am sure we can sort it out." This is a 'can-do' attitude and it offers many advantages.

Firstly, it will stretch you, which will help you learn and grow. Secondly, it will plant you firmly in the minds of bosses, colleagues and clients as someone with a positive, problem-solving attitude. Not somebody who emits negative doom and gloom. You may not know how to solve the problem right away but, given time, you will.

According to author Shawn Achor, it's like looking beyond the proverbial 'glass half empty, glass half full' rhetoric and saying that neither matters. Why? Because you've spotted the pitcher that can be used to refill the glass anyway. He calls this the 'happiness advantage' because not only does it make one feel better about life in general, but it also greatly benefits business outcomes.

In Shawn's first book, *Before Happiness*, he argues that before you can be happy you need to be positive. Being positive makes you happier, and happiness is a performance driver.

Personally, I became happier as I became more successful. In the beginning, I was so concerned about being not very good that I didn't have any space for happiness.

However, I remained positive.

People who have a positive mindset in the face of challenge perform better on nearly every level: productivity, creativity, engagement.

In one piece of academic research that Shawn conducted with three other colleagues, he found that "happy employees have, on average, 31 per cent higher productivity; their sales are 37 per cent higher; their creativity is three times higher". Sounds like a good advantage to me.

The trick is not to use success as a happiness driver but the other way around. Do not think, like most people, "I will be happy when I get that promotion". Otherwise, as soon as you get it you will have to move the target again because success is fleeting. So too is happiness based on success. When you're positive you don't need outside stimulus to influence the outcome. Your positive mindset will do that for you.

One of the quickest ways to test your level of positivity at work is to look at the way you approach problems. Do you throw your hands up in despair and try to find someone else to solve them for you? Or do you look for the pitcher?

I learnt to do the latter because I once had a boss who constantly said, "Don't bring me problems, bring me answers." Later, I said the same thing to people who worked for me. Don't say, "Boss, we have a problem", say, "Boss, we have a problem, but I think there are at least three ways to solve it." Tell your boss what they are, and then ask him or her which one they think is best.

One of the big things I learnt about problems – and, believe me, I have had to deal with my fair share – is that what might seem like a huge, looming puzzle at the time, rarely looks like one six months later. As Margaret Thatcher once remarked "Quiet, calm deliberation untangles every knot." Time is a great solver of problems. Taking the time to write down problems will often help lead to a solution.

A can-do attitude will call for what psychologist Carol Dweck describes as a 'growth mindset'. Remember, even the simplest belief will profoundly affect what we achieve in life. If you believe there is no solution to a problem, you won't even try to look for one – let alone find one. People with this 'can't-do' attitude avoid situations and opportunities if they believe there is a high chance of failure. But in actual fact, by that very omission they are guaranteeing their own failure, because they are avoiding tasks that will provide them with the opportunity to grow. As Huw Wheldon, a former managing director of the BBC, once said, "the idea is not to avoid failure at any cost, the idea is to give triumph a chance".

With a growth mindset you will seize opportunities to learn and grow; you will not shy away from tough tasks; you will not avoid failure at any cost. You may not have the skills or experience you need today, but you will have them tomorrow. Your positive attitude will see to that.

Let me give you a word of warning, though; I am not suggesting that you rush willy-nilly into tasks without knowing what's involved. You may not know the answer right now, but you should understand fully the problem and what it might involve to solve it. And always be ready to learn how to do something you've never done before. It can usually be done. If you don't know how, somebody else will. You've just got to find that somebody.

Exercise 13: Adopt a 'can-do' attitude

1. Be willing to help. Remember, if you don't know how to solve a problem you can always find someone who does.

2. Practice congruence. This means to act as though you're already the kind of person you want to become. The more you do, the more natural it will become to you.

Afterword

Writing this book has been cathartic. Before I started, I had never stopped to think why I did what I did. Why did I become an advertising man? Why did I leave a successful career with a successful agency, and jump in and start a new one? How did I find the courage to buy it out, despite complete opposition from my bosses? And then, how did I manage to sell it successfully just 10 months after our biggest client went bust owing us some £4 million?

Looking back at those first 15 years, all of the keys I have identified for you are important, but three were pivotal.

Firstly, I never stopped learning. From my earliest school days I had always found understanding new things difficult. I could not read until I was seven. Nowadays, I would have been diagnosed as severely dyslexic. As a result, throughout my life, I have always had to work harder to learn new things. I now realise that this was in fact an advantage. When I started work, having to learn a myriad of new hard and soft skills was familiar to me. I just got on with it.

Years later, the burgeoning insights of Neuroscience have proven that learning cognitively demanding tasks will never be quick. It always takes time. Neurons need time to connect, years in fact, but once they have connected, they stay connected.

By the way, one of the joys of getting older but still working, is you realise that you never stop learning, and that the acquisition of new knowledge and new insights is one of the things that makes for a worthwhile life.

So start learning and never stop.

Secondly, not everything will come easily, nor is it likely to be straightforward. Throughout my life there have been countless occasions when I could have either bolted, or tried to sort something out in the wrong way. I learnt that if you apply yourself most things can be sorted.

So you will need to learn the value of 'grit'. If you come up against a situation, which is truly hopeless, or a role where you have a horrible boss, then by all means, bail out as fast as you can. However, time and time again I have come to realise that you need to stick at something until it comes good. When I was hiring I always looked for instances of where people had overcome problems. Resilience is a much underrated trait but one which will always be in demand by employers.

Grit is good.

Thirdly, if you want to learn as much as you can, as fast as you can, work for a great company. You will learn so much more quickly. Better people will surround you; you will probably have better bosses, who know what they want, from both clients and staff. You won't have to play endless political games and it will be much more satisfying and enjoyable, even if the work is tougher.

It's important for all young graduates, once they have navigated the first years of work and understand how their industry works, to select the best companies in their field, I was lucky enough to be employed by the best advertising agency in the world at the tender age of 23; I was 25 before I began to realise how great it was; and 28, fully five years after I had started at CDP that it eventually dawned on me that it was simply the best. By then I realised I had to forge my own destiny and not ride on the coat tails of others.

I urge every young graduate to seek the same opportunities as I did. You will never regret it.

And always keep your journal up to date. It will eventually form part of the diary of your life!

So now this book is finished, writing it has proved to be instructive. I have rewritten it four times and had to have a lot of help along the way. I simply could not have done it by myself.

Maybe that's another key? Surround yourself with people who can help you! Good luck and enjoy your journey.

Bibliography

Achor, S. (2013). *Before Happiness: The 5 Hidden Keys to Achieving Success, Spreading Happiness, and Sustaining Positive Change*. Crown Publishing Group.

Achor, S. (2012). *Positive Intelligence*. [Online]. Available at: https://hbr.org/2012/01/positive-intelligence

Achor, S. (2010). *The Happiness Advantage: The Seven Principles that Fuel Success and Performance at Work*. Virgin Books.

Achor, S. *What You Need To Do Before Experiencing Happiness*. [Online]. Available at: http://www.forbes.com/

Barker, E. *How do you find the best mentor for you?* [Online]. Available at: http://www.bakadesuyo.com/

BrainyQuote.com 'V. S. Naipaul'. Xplore Inc, 30 June 2016. [Online]. Available at: http://www.brainyquote.com/quotes/quotes/v/vsnaipau475126.html

Buckingham, M., Clifton, D. O., (2004). *Now, Discover Your Strengths*. Simon & Schuster UK

Colvin, G. (2008). *Talent is Overrated*. Penguin Group.

Coyle, D. (2012). *The Little Book of Talent: 52 Tips for Improving Your Skills*. RandomHouse.

Cuddy, A. (2016). *Presence*. Orion.

Dealtry, R. (2004). *The Savvy Learner. Journal of Workplace Learning*, 16(1/2), pp. 101–109.

Del Giudice, M. *Grit Trumps Talent and IQ: A Story Every Parent (and Educator) Should Read*. National Geographic [Online]. Available at: http://news.nationalgeographic.com/